S

small worlds

# A

# DEAD

# LOG

**Jen Green**

**CRABTREE**
Publishing Company

# Crabtree Publishing Company

350 Fifth Avenue
Suite 3308
New York, NY 10118

360 York Road, R.R.4
Niagara-on-the-Lake
Ontario LOS 1J0

**Co-ordinating editor:** Ellen Rodger
**Commissioning editor:** Anne O'Daly
**Editor:** Clare Oliver
**Designer:** Joan Curtis
**Picture researcher:** Christine Lalla
**Consultants:** Staff of the Natural History Museum, London
and David T. Brown PhD

**Illustrator:** Peter Bull
**Photographs:** Jim Hallett/BBC Natural History Unit p 26*m*; Neil Lucas/BBC Natural History Unit p 14*b*; Premaphotos/BBC Natural History Unit p 18*t*; Lynn M Stone/BBC Natural History Unit pp 10*t,b*; David Welling/BBC Natural History Unit p 12*b*; J Brackenbury/Bruce Coleman Limited p 23*b*; Jules Cowan/Bruce Coleman Limited p 4*m*; Jeff Foott/Bruce Coleman Limited pp 15*t*, 29; Christer Fredriksson/Bruce Coleman Limited, front and back cover, pp 3, 9; Bob Glover/Bruce Coleman Limited p 8*m*; Peter A Hinchliffe/Bruce Coleman Limited pp 7*br*, 27; Stephen J Krasemann/Bruce Coleman p 5; Wayne Lankinen/Bruce Coleman Limited p 13; Michael Price/Bruce Coleman Limited p 1, 24*bl*; Andrew Purcell/Bruce Coleman Limited pp 6, 24*t*; Marie Read/Bruce Coleman Limited p 11; Dr Frieder Sauer/Bruce Coleman Limited p 26*t*; Kim Taylor/Bruce Coleman Limited pp 18*m*, 19, 21*b*; Imagebank, front cover, pp 8*t*, 12*t*; NHPA pp 15*b*, 17, 20, 21*t*, 22, 23*t*, 31*b*; Harry Smith Horticultural Collection pp4*t*, 7*bl*, 14*t*, 16, 25, 31*t*.

Created and produced by
**Brown Partworks Ltd**

First edition 1999
10 9 8 7 6 5 4 3 2 1

Copyright © 1999 Brown Partworks Ltd

CATALOGING-IN-PUBLICATION DATA

Green, Jen, 1955-
    A dead log / Jen Green. — 1st ed.
    p. cm. — (Small worlds)
Includes index.
    SUMMARY: Describes the various creatures and plants that live in, on, or under a dead log.
    ISBN 0-7787-0136-0 (rlb)
    ISBN 0-7787-0150-6 (pbk.)
    1. Forest ecology—Juvenile literature. 2. Forest animals—Habitat—Juvenile literature. 3. Trees—Ecology—Juvenile literature. 4. Dead trees—Juvenile literature. [1. Forest ecology. 2. Ecology. 3. Dead trees.] I. Title. II. Series: Small worlds.
    QH541.5.F6 G74 1999
    577.3—dc21

LC 98-51707
CIP
AC

Printed in Singapore

# Contents

# Forest home

**Wherever trees grow, you will often find dead logs. Although the log itself is lifeless, it is home to many plants and animals.**

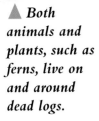

▲ *Both animals and plants, such as ferns, live on and around dead logs.*

▶ *Forests of spruce and pine are found in the north. These trees are evergreens, which means they do not shed their leaves.*

Around the world, there are many different types of forests. Near the Equator, there are hot, steamy rain forests. In the far north, forests of spruce and pine grow. Each type of forest is home to its own wildlife. In this book you will meet the amazing plants and animals that live in and around a dead log in a North American broad-leaf forest.

▶ *Broad-leaf trees shed their leaves in fall then grow new ones the next spring.*

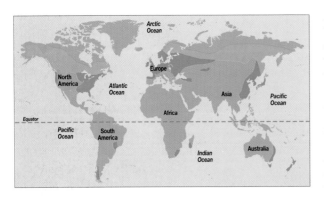

◀ *On this map, broad-leaf forests are shown in red, and coniferous forests in purple.*

# Life in a dead log

**A living tree is home to many different creatures. When the tree dies and crashes to the ground, a different set of animals and plants moves in.**

Dead logs and fallen branches litter the ground in every natural forest. This dead wood may look untidy, but one-fifth of all woodland creatures would lose their homes if it were cleared away. Different kinds of animals and plants make their homes in various parts of the log, like people living in different parts of a large city.

The plants and animals that live on a dead log start from the outside and move inward, as the log slowly rots. Fungi and wood-boring insects make their way underneath the bark and into the wood. As the wood decays, more animals tunnel deep inside. After 20 years or more, the log crumbles away, and the animals move to a fresh log.

### Under the bark
All sorts of small animals, including beetles, centipedes, and sow bugs, tunnel and feed under the bark.

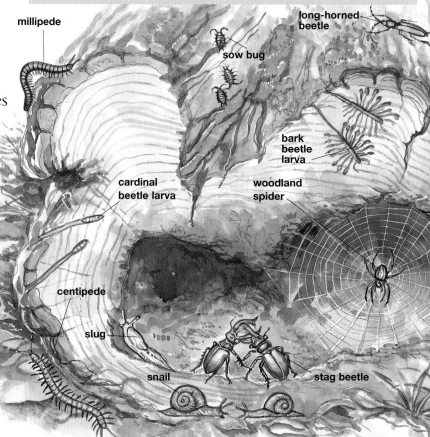

millipede

long-horned beetle

sow bug

bark beetle larva

cardinal beetle larva

woodland spider

centipede

slug

snail

stag beetle

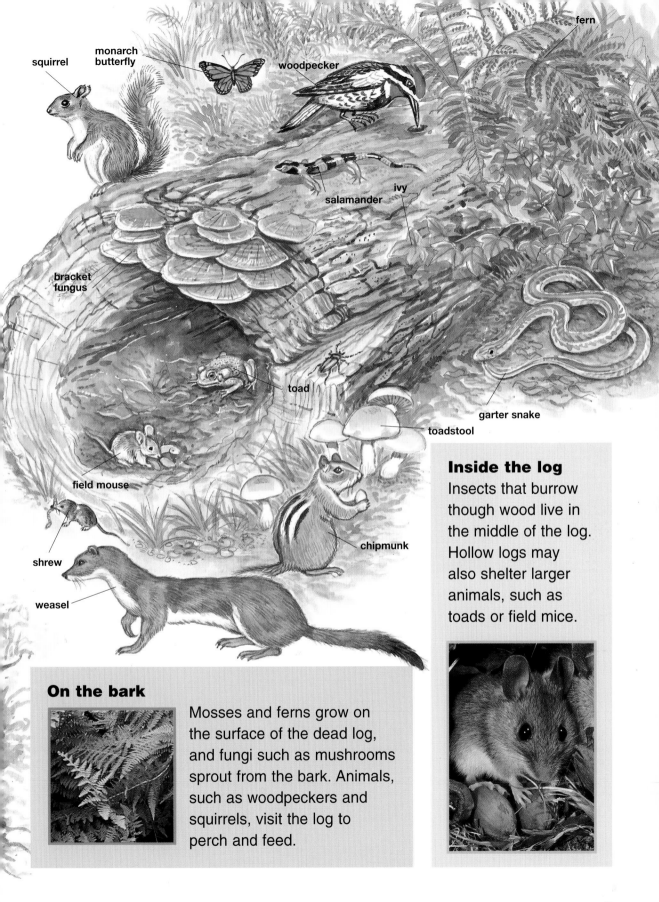

squirrel

monarch
butterfly

fern

woodpecker

salamander

ivy

bracket
fungus

toad

garter snake

toadstool

field mouse

chipmunk

shrew

weasel

## Inside the log
Insects that burrow
though wood live in
the middle of the log.
Hollow logs may
also shelter larger
animals, such as
toads or field mice.

## On the bark
Mosses and ferns grow on
the surface of the dead log,
and fungi such as mushrooms
sprout from the bark. Animals,
such as woodpeckers and
squirrels, visit the log to
perch and feed.

# On the bark

The outside of the log attracts wildlife first, because it makes a good lookout for animals wary of predators. Soon, all sorts of animals and plants move in.

*▲ Chipmunks make a chipping noise if danger approaches. This warns other chipmunks to beware.*

*▶ The gray squirrel stands upright on the log as it eats, so that it can keep an eye out for danger.*

Many woodland creatures visit the dead log and use it as a safe perch. Squirrels and chipmunks sit on their hind legs on logs or tree stumps, nibbling at seeds and nuts. They have a better view from here than from on the ground. From this lookout post, they keep a careful watch for other animals and birds. At the first hint of danger, they dart up the nearest tree trunk and leap to safety among the branches.

*▶ In many forests, rangers, the people who look after the forest, leave dead logs and branches lying on the ground to encourage wildlife.*

### The weasel

Squirrels and chipmunks are plant eaters, feeding on shoots and buds as well as nuts and berries. In contrast, the weasel is a **predator**. By day and night, weasels creep or bound through the forest, tracking small creatures such as mice and voles. Predators also use fallen logs and tree stumps as lookouts, standing up on their hind legs to take a good look around for **prey**.

## Spot the weasel

Many woodland animals are colored to blend in with their surroundings. This disguise, or **camouflage**, helps them to hide from predators or to hunt for prey.

During the summer, the weasel's brown-gray fur blends in with the tree bark, making the animal hard to spot. In winter, it sheds its summer coat and grows warm, thick fur. This coat is white and is a perfect camouflage against the snowy landscape.

## In cold blood

Weasels and squirrels are warm-blooded animals, or **mammals**, but cold-blooded animals use the log as a perch, too. These include **reptiles**, such as snakes and lizards, and insects, such as butterflies. The body temperatures of these creatures depend on their surroundings. They need a spot where they can bask in the sun to warm up after a cold night.

The northern brown snake is a common woodland reptile, but you might miss it. It is less than 12 inches (30 cm) long and is small for a snake. Garter snakes are twice as long. Brown snakes and garter snakes are harmless to humans. These snakes feast on the insects, earthworms, and **amphibians** that live around the log.

▲ *The northern brown snake's brown coloring helps it to hide in the leaf litter on the forest floor.*

You may be lucky enough to spot a monarch butterfly stopping off for a rest on a log. Each fall, these amazing insects fly from their summer home in Canada all the way down to Mexico, their winter home, a distance of more than 2,175 miles (3,500 km).

## Delicious grub

Many insects make their home in the bark of a fallen log. Beetles, ants, and flies crawl over the rough surface in search of food and shelter. They lay their eggs in cracks and crevices. Soon the log is a hunting ground for animals that eat insects.

▲ *In the early morning, butterflies such as this monarch bask on the log with outstretched wings.*

▼ *Birds, such as this hairy woodpecker, hunt for grubs in the bark. The birds use their stout beaks to dig for insects.*

## Woody woodpecker

The woodpecker is a bird that likes to make a meal of insects. It pokes its beak into the bark of trees and uses its long tongue to slurp up its juicy prey. The woodpecker should feel right at home on a dead log. After all, it hollows out its nest in the dead wood of an old tree.

## The fantastic flicker

The flicker is another type of woodpecker. It has a specially curved beak for teasing out its favorite food, ants. Many birds avoid eating ants because their bodies produce acid, which makes them taste bitter. The flicker's saliva contains a special chemical that is slightly alkaline (the opposite of acidic). This chemical destroys the ants' acid in the flicker's mouth.

*▲ At 13 inches (33 cm) long, the flicker is slightly larger than the hairy woodpecker.*

## A green carpet

As the log begins to rot, the wood soaks up water like a sponge. Before long, moisture-loving mosses and ferns cover the bark. Mosses are small plants without stems or roots. They form thick, spongy mats of vegetation that spread along the bark.

Ferns look very different. They have long shoots called fronds, with graceful, curling leaves. Like all plants, ferns make their own food by using sunlight. The green coloring in their stems and leaves, called chlorophyll, uses the energy in sunlight to make food for the plant. This process is called **photosynthesis**.

▲ *Mosses live on the bark of dead logs and even fallen twigs or branches.*

▼ *Ferns are some of the oldest plants on Earth. They grow well in damp forests.*

*Fern spores are made in little sacs called sporangia, underneath the leaves. If you lift up a fern frond, you might see the sacs.*

Ferns and mosses do not reproduce by making seeds, as most plants do. Instead, they release special cells called spores, which develop into new plants under the right conditions.

*Bracket fungi look like tiny shelves sprouting from the bark of tree stumps or logs. Unlike mushrooms and toadstools, they are hard and may last for several years.*

## Fabulous fungi

Fungi are neither plants nor animals, but a separate group of living things. Unlike green plants, they cannot make their own food through photosynthesis. Instead, they feed on rotting plant matter, such as fallen logs, or on animal remains in soil.

## Fungi fodder

To feed on the log, the fungi sends a network of tiny threads called hyphae through the wood. The threads release chemicals that dissolve the wood so the fungi can digest it.

The bark of living trees contains chemicals that prevent the growth of fungi. Dead or decaying trees no longer produce these chemicals, so fungi sprout in the dead wood, wherever their spores land. You are most likely to see sprouting fungi in fall, especially if it is wet and rainy.

Some kinds of mushrooms can be eaten, but many are very poisonous. It is often difficult to tell edible from poisonous species, so you should only eat mushrooms that have been identified by an expert.

**FANTASTIC FACTS**

● There are over 70,000 different kinds of fungi.

● Yeasts, molds, and mildews are all types of fungi.

● Mushrooms often grow in circles, which are called fairy rings.

# The hidden life of fungi

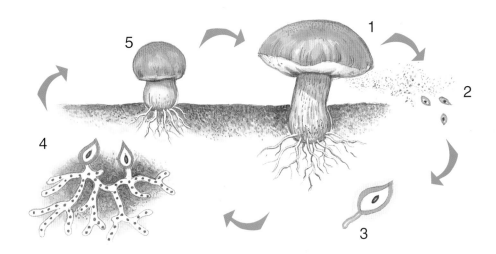

Fungi reproduce by forming fruit bodies on the surface of the log. The fruit bodies are the bracket fungi, mushrooms, or toadstools that you notice sprouting from the log (1). Fruit bodies produce millions of spores, which drift away on the wind (2). The spores shoot out tiny threads (3), called hyphae, that make an underground web. When part of the web reaches the web of another spore, the two mate and join together (4). After mating, the joined webs can produce a new young fruit body that pushes up to the surface (5), and the whole process begins all over again.

# Under the bark

Under the bark of a dead log, bugs are safe from predators and protected from the weather. The log provides food and moisture.

*▲ If danger threatens, the sow bug rolls its armored body into a tight ball.*

*▶ Hidden beneath the rotting bark, a sow bug sheds its old skin. The cast-off skin looks like a sow bug costume!*

Many insects and bugs live inside the dead log all year round. Sow bugs are found in large numbers under or inside dead logs. Sow bugs are not insects. They are distant relatives of crabs and lobsters. They lose water easily, so they like the cool, damp conditions of the log. They rest in the log during the day, to avoid the heat of the sun.

*▶ Larvae, such as these stag and tanner beetle grubs, eat their way through the dead log's wood.*

## Boring beetles

Beetles are insects, but, like sow bugs, they protect their soft bodies with a hard outer case. The case is like a tiny suit of armor. Beetles have an extra protection. Their hard front wings fold over their bodies to protect the delicate hind wings, which they use for flying.

There are thousands of different kinds of beetle. Some feed on leaves and other plant matter. Others hunt and kill other small bugs for food. Some feed on dead wood and eat their way through fallen logs.

## Stupendous stags

Stag beetles are wood-burrowers whose larvae spend up to five years feeding inside the log. As adults, they continue to live around rotting logs, feeding on sap. Stag beetles are named for their

▶ *These two male stag beetles are fighting over a female. Each tries to toss the other into the air and then bash it to the ground.*

*Adult long-horned beetles do not eat wood. They sip the sweet nectar of flowers. Their larvae burrow inside dead logs and feed there on the wood for years.*

fierce fighting jaws, which look like antlers. These are mainly used when the adult males want to attract females. Each male tries to frighten other males away, because the winner is the one that the female mates with.

## Tunneling through

Fire-colored beetles breed in dead wood, too. Once the female has mated, she digs into the wood and lays her eggs. When they hatch, the larvae look very different from their mother. They have long, fat bodies and no wings. The grubs stay in the log, eating through the wood, until they are ready to change into adults with wings. They then bore, or drill, their way to freedom and fly away, leaving small, round exit holes in the wood. The larvae feed on all kinds of wood, not just dead logs. Sometimes they can be found in wooden houses and furniture!

*These fire-colored beetle larvae will stay in the log for up to three years.*

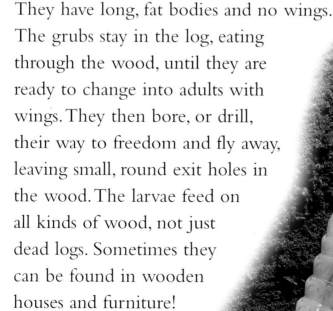

## Bark and bite

Bark beetles are often the first bugs to move into a dead log. They loosen the bark and speed up the decaying process of the log. The female bores a little tunnel in the wood and lays her eggs in it. Her larvae burrow outward from this central passage, making a star-shaped pattern in the wood.

*Most bark beetles specialize in one type of wood. These patterns have been bored by elm bark beetles in elm wood. The dark bits are where fungi are growing on the walls of the tunnels.*

## Laying eggs

The horntail is a type of wasp that bores deep into the log. Its horn-shaped egg-layer looks like a stinger, but it is harmless. Eggs laid in the log hatch and become wood-eating larvae. The ichneumon is another fly with a long egg-layer, which it uses to drill into wood. The

◀ *The horntail drills into the wood with its long egg-layer.*

▼ *In winter, ichneumons go into a deep sleep inside the log. This sleep is called hibernation.*

ichneumon lays its egg right on the horntail grub. No one knows just how the ichneumon finds the grub in the wood. When the ichneumon larva hatches, it feeds on the fat, juicy grub, and eventually kills it. All of these wood-boring beetles and flies help dead wood to rot. Once the timber has decayed, other bugs move in.

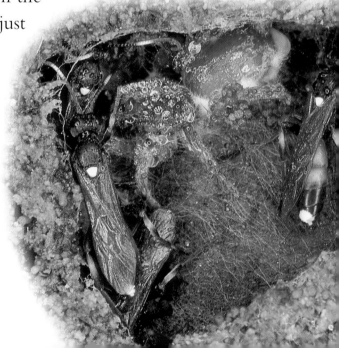

▶ *The word "centipede" means one hundred legs, but a centipede may have as few as 30 legs or as many as 300 legs!*

## On the march

Centipedes and millipedes are long, wriggling animals, called arthropods, that live in the holes in logs that are drilled by beetles. The centipede is **nocturnal**. It hides inside the log by day and comes out at night to hunt. It is a fierce predator, catching worms, slugs, spiders, and even other centipedes for food. It chases after its prey on its many legs and paralyzes victims with a bite from its poisoned jaws. Millipedes are relatives of centipedes, but they move less quickly. They are too slow to chase and catch other creatures for food. Instead, they feed on decaying leaves and rotten wood.

◀ *The millipede's many legs move in waves as it travels.*

# Who am I?

A lot of the animals in a dead log look similar, with their jointed bodies and many legs. To identify them, look at the body shape and count the legs and see if there are any wings.

Many adult insects have at least six legs, and some also have wings. Spiders have eight legs and are wingless. Sow bugs have gray, oval bodies and seven pairs of legs. Centipedes, millipedes, and earthworms have long, wingless bodies divided into many sections. Centipedes have a pair of legs on each body segment, while millipedes have two pairs. Earthworms have no legs at all!

# Inside the log

Over time, wood-boring insects and fungi break down the log. The hollow log that they leave behind makes a perfect hiding place for forest wildlife.

▲ *A female mouse can have over 50 babies a year. The young mice need a safe home, but many are still eaten by predators.*

▶ *Shrews sometimes shelter inside fallen logs. They also visit logs to hunt worms and insects.*

Small furry animals such as mice sometimes build their nests inside dry hollow logs. The nest is a warm place to rest and sleep and a safe home for the young. At first, the newborn mice are bald, blind, and helpless. But they grow up quickly, fed by their mother's milk. After two weeks, the babies have grown hair and can see and hear well. A few weeks more, and they are ready to leave the nest and look after themselves.

▶ *Field mice drag dry leaves and grasses into the dead log to build a cosy nest. They will spend the winter in the log, living off their food stores of nuts and seeds.*

Shrews sometimes have their litter inside a hollow log. Each litter can contain up to 10 tiny babies. It is important for a shrew to be near the food it eats, such as insects and dead animals. The shrew has to have a meal every few hours, otherwise it dies. Shrews eat more than their own weight in food every day!

### Seeking shelter

Toads and salamanders search for moist places to live and often burrow in or under rotten logs. These animals are amphibians, which means that they are equally at home in water and on land. They need damp conditions because their skins are not waterproof and do not keep moisture in.

Toads and salamanders are mainly nocturnal. They hide and rest in their burrows by day and come out to feed at night. The toad eats snails, sow bugs, and insects. Salamanders prefer worms and slugs.

Toads and salamanders return to the pond to lay their eggs. The young toads (tadpoles) and young salamanders (larvae) live in the water and have

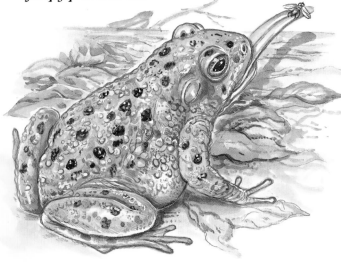

▼ *A toad shoots out its long, sticky tongue to capture a juicy fly in mid-air.*

gills like fish. They feed and grow in the water. In a few months they develop legs and lungs. Then, the toads and salamanders crawl out of the pond and find a hollow log where they begin their lives on land.

▲ *A hollow log makes a dark, damp home for this salamander.*

## The web of life

All the animals that live in the dead log are part of a great web of life in the forest. Mice get all the food they need from seeds, fruit, and other parts of plants. Many insects, such as millipedes, are also plant eaters. Other small creatures, such as centipedes, are meat eaters. They feed on plant eaters and, in turn, are eaten by larger animals such as shrews and birds. The biggest, strongest hunters, such as owls and weasels, prey on birds, shrews, and mice. The links between all these animals make a food chain. When the big predators die, their bodies rot, and meat-eating insects feed on *them*! The cycle begins again.

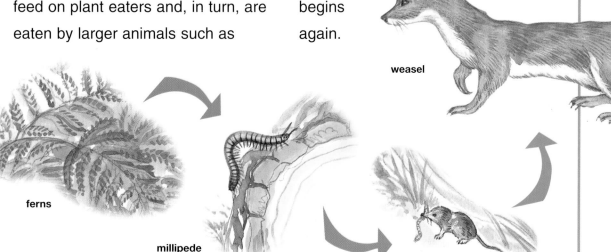

ferns

millipede

shrew

weasel

# Be a log detective

**Look at dead logs, or even fallen twigs, in your local park. You could work out the age of the tree when it fell or see what sorts of animals have moved in.**

The animals that live in dead logs are delicate. Make a viewing jar so that you can study them without hurting them, and always return them to the log.

You will need a small plastic jar with a lid. Ask an adult to pierce two holes in the lid, each just big enough to fit a straw through. Now take two wide, bendable straws and put one in each hole as shown. Seal them in position with modeling clay. Tape a tiny square of muslin over one of the straws, then fit the lid on the jar.

To collect insects from a log, put the muslin-capped straw in your mouth, and aim the end of the other straw at the log. Now suck, to draw the creatures inside the jar. See if you can find some of the bugs you have read about in this book. Why not

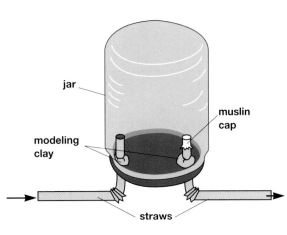

jar

muslin cap

modeling clay

straws

▲ *The muslin will stop you from sucking any bugs into your mouth.*

▶ *You can find out the age of a fallen or chopped-down tree. Each year that the tree was alive, it grew a new layer of wood beneath the bark. So each year of its life is represented by a ring. Count the rings, and you can tell how many years the tree lived!*

keep a log "log" to record what you see? Visit the same log at different times of the day or year and write about the creatures you find there in a special notebook. Once you start looking, you will soon see that a dead log is a small world that is bursting with life.

▼ *Some insects are too big to catch in a jar. You can study earwigs and how they behave just by standing very still next to the log.*

# Words to know

**amphibian** An animal that lives both on land and in the water.
**camouflage** Colors and patterns that help an animal to blend in with its surroundings.
**gill** A feathery organ used for breathing underwater.
**larva** An immature insect.
**mammal** A warm-blooded, hairy animal that suckles its young.
**nocturnal** Describes an animal that sleeps or rests by day and is active at night.
**photosynthesis** Process by which plants make their food, using the energy in sunlight.
**predator** An animal that hunts other animals for food.
**prey** An animal that is eaten by another animal.
**reptile** A cold-blooded, scaly, air-breathing animal.

# Index